I0832649

A VOYAGE

TO

THE FORTUNATE ISLES,

ETC.

BY

MRS. S. M. B. PIATT,

Author of "A Woman's Poems."

BOSTON:
JAMES R. OSGOOD AND COMPANY,
LATE TICKNOR & FIELDS, AND FIELDS, OSGOOD & CO.
1874.

CONTENTS.

	PAGE
A Voyage to the Fortunate Isles,	1
There Was a Rose,	14
Gifts of a Dream,	17
If I Were a Queen,	20
Their Two Fortunes,	29
Sometime,	32
The Dead Fairies,	36
The Order for Her Portrait,	38
"I Want it Yesterday,"	41
Marble or Dust?	43
Their Lost Picture,	46
Seeing Through Tears,	48
To-Morrow,	50
Sweetness of Bitterness,	53
A Woman's Answer,	57
The Favorite Child,	62
The Clothes of a Ghost,	64
Flight,	68
Beatrice Cenci,	71
Over in Kentucky,	74
An East-Indian Fairy Story,	78
Baby or Bird?	80
Say the Sweet Words,	82

PAGE
A Butterfly's Message, ... 83
Leaving Love, ... 87
The Black Princess, ... 90
One Poet's Silence, ... 94
Her Simile, ... 96
A Prettier Book, ... 97
A Precious Seeing, ... 101
The Funeral of a Doll, ... 104
A Parting Gift of Youth, ... 108
Crying for the Moon, ... 112
Aunt Annie, ... 114
The Palace-Burner, ... 119
Love-Stories, ... 123
His Fairy Godmother, ... 128
Why Should We Care? 132
At the Play, ... 136
"I Wish that I Could Go," 139
A Life in a Mirror, ... 145
When the Full Moon's Light is Burning, ... 148
Our Old and New Landlords, ... 149
A Doubt, ... 154
This World, ... 157
The Flight of the Children, ... 162
A Masked Ball, ... 165
A Woman's Birthday, ... 170
His Share and Mine, ... 173
Life or Love, ... 176
The Dead Book, ... 180

A VOYAGE TO THE FORTUNATE ISLES,

ETC.

A VOYAGE TO THE FORTUNATE ISLES.

THE FABLE OF A HOUSEHOLD.

"YES, but I fear to leave the shore.
So fierce, so shadowy, so cold,
Deserts of water lie before—
Whose secrets night has never told,
Save in close whispers to the dead.
I fear," one vaguely said.

One answered: "Will you waver here?
As wild and lonesome as the things

Which hold their wet nests, year by year,
In these poor rocks, are we. Their wings
Grow restless—wherefore not our feet?
That which is strange is sweet."

"That which we know is sweeter yet.
Do we not love the near Earth more
Than the far Heaven? Does not Regret
Walk with us, always, from the door
That shuts behind us, though we leave
Not much to make us grieve?"

"Why fret me longer, when you know
Our hands with thorny toil are torn?

Scant bread and bitter, heat and snow,
  Rude garments, souls too blind and worn
To climb to Christ for comfort: these
    Are here. And there—the Seas.

"True, our great Lord will let us drink
  At some wild springs, and even take
A few slight dew-flowers. But, I think,
  He cares not how our hearts may ache.
He comes not to the peasant's hut
    To learn—the door is shut.

"Oh, He is an hard Master. Still
  In His rough fields, for piteous hire,

To break dry clods is not my will.
  I thank Him that my arms can tire.
Let thistles henceforth grow like grain,
    To mock His sun and rain.

"Others He lifts to high estate—
  Others, no peers of yours or mine.
He folds them in a silken fate,
  Casts pearls before them—oh, the swine!
Drugs them with wine, veils them with lace;
    And gives us this mean place."

"Well. May there not be butterflies
  That lift with weary wings the air;

That loathe the foreign sun, which lies
On all their colors like despair;
That glitter, home-sick for the form
And lost sleep of the worm?"

"Hush—see the ship. It comes at last,"
She whispered, through forlornest smiles:
"How brave it is! It sails so fast.
It takes us to the Fortunate Isles.
Come." Then the heart's great silence drew
Like Death around the Two.

Death-like it was—through pain and doubt,
To leave their world at once and go,

Pale, mute, and even unconscious, out
  Through dimness toward some distant Glow,
That might be but Illusion caught
    In the fine net of Thought.

As ghosts, led by a ghostly sleep—
  Followed by Life, a breathless dream—
Out in eternal dusk that keep
  Their way somewhere, these Two did seem,
Till the sea-moon climbed to her place
    And looked in each still face.

"The worm," she waking said, "must long
  To put on beauty and to fly,

But"———coming toward them sad and strong,
There was a little double cry.
"What hurts the children? They should rest,
In such a floating nest."

"Oh, Mother, look—we all are gone.
Our house is swimming in the sea.
It will not stop. It keeps right on.
How far away we all must be!
The wind has blown it from the cliff.
It rocks us like a skiff.

"We all will drown but Baby. He
Is in his pretty grave so far.

He has to sleep till Judgment. We
  Must sink where all the sailors are,
Who used to die, when storms would come,
    Away off from their home."

"Lie still, you foolish yellow heads.
  This is a ship. We're sailing." "Where?"
"Go nestle in your little beds.
  Be quiet. We shall soon be there."
"Where?" "Why, it is not many miles."
    "Where?" "To the Fortunate Isles."

"Home is the best. Oh, what a light!
  God must be looking in the sea.

It is His glass. He makes it bright
All over with His face. And He
Is angry. He is talking loud
Out of that broken cloud.

"The men all hear Him, in the ropes:
He's telling them the ship must go.
They'd better climb to Him." Pale Hopes
Looked from each wretched breast, to know
If somewhere, through the shattered night,
One sail could be in sight.

And Two, who waited, dying slow,
Said, clinging to their desperate calm:

"We had not thought such wind could blow
Out of the warm leaves of the palm.
Strange, with the Fortunate Isles so nigh—
Strange, cruel, thus to die."

"The Fortunate Isles?" one other cried;
"You knew we were not sailing there?
They lie far back across the tide.
Their cliffs are gray and wet and bare;
And quiet people in their soil
Are still content to toil.

"Toward shining snakes, toward fair dumb birds,
Toward Fever hiding in the spice,

We voyaged." But his tropic words
  Dropped icy upon hearts of ice.
The lonesome gulf to which they passed
    Had shown the Truth at last.

That wavering glare, the drowning see
  With phantoms of their life therein,
Flashed on them both. Yet mostly she
  Felt all her sorrow, all her sin,
And learned, most bitterly, how dear
    Their crags and valleys were.

Their home, whose dim wet windows stared
  Through drops of brine, like eyes through tears;

The blue ground-blossoms that had cared
To creep about their feet for years;
And their one grave so deep, so small—
Sinking, they saw them all!

To leave the Fortunate Isles, away
On the other side of the world, and sail
Still farther from them, day by day,
Dreaming to find them; and to fail
In knowing, till the very last,
They held one's own sweet Past:

Such lot was theirs. Such lot will be,
Ah, much I fear me, yours and mine.

Because our air is cold, and we
  See Summer in some mirage shine,
We leave the Fortunate Isles behind,
    The Fortunate Isles to find.

THERE WAS A ROSE.

"THERE was a rose," she said,
"Like other roses, perhaps, to you.
Nine years ago it was faint and red,
Away in the cold dark dew,
On the dwarf bush where it grew.

"Never any rose before
Was like that rose, very well I know;

Never another rose any more
  Will blow as that rose did blow,
  When the wet wind shook it so.

"'What do I want?'—Ah, what?
  Why, I want that rose, that wee one rose,
Only that rose. And that rose is not
  Anywhere just now? . . . God knows
  Where all the old sweetness goes.

"I want that rose so much;
  I would take the world back there to the night
Where I saw it blush in the grass, to touch
  It once in that fair fall light,
  And only once, if I might.

"But a million marching men
From the North and the South would arise?
And the dead—would have to die again?
And the women's widowed cries
Would trouble anew the skies?

"No matter. I would not care;
Were it not better that this should be?
The sorrow of many the many bear,—
Mine is too heavy for me.
And I want that rose, you see!"

GIFTS OF A DREAM.

ONE whispered through my sleep:
"I bring a statue here with me,
Worth half the world. No queen has one to keep,
So precious. Wake and see.

"I also bring a vine,
To plant by cottage windows—one
Whose brood of blossoms may be fair and fine
As ever pleased the sun.

"He sent them, Dear, to you
  Who loves you with a love divine.
Arise and look, and choose one of the two,
  Or let the choice be mine."

I reached my eager arm
  To catch the marble: heard a moan,
And knew my heavy hand had crushed the charm,
  And left—some dead white stone!

He murmured, with a kiss,
  "Poor child," and laughed the lightest laugh,
"The statue was worth half the world, but this
  Is worth the other half."

And left the rose in dew.

Now, gathering buds, and bright with bees,
It fills my life with honey. Dreams come true—
Such lovely dreams as these.

IF I WERE A QUEEN.

"BUT if you were a Queen?" you said.
Well, then I think my favorite page
Should have a yellow, restless head,
And be just your own pretty age.
So sweet in violet velvet, he
Should tend my butterflies in herds,
Or help that belted knight, the bee,
Win honey, or make little birds
Some little songs to sing for me—
If I were a Queen.

A Queen—you saw one sitting by
  A tall man in a picture? Well.
He had a harp? You need not try—
  Her name is one you can not tell.
And so you wonder if I could
  Be Isolt, then? Not she, I fear,
To save Sir Tristram of the Wood
  And all his tripping silver deer;
For it were better to be good,
          If I were a Queen.

Nor Guinevere———You ask, would I
  Be Queen Elizabeth? Oh! no;
For, then, should I not have to die
  And leave, all hanging in a row,

Two thousand dresses? Could I bear
  To sit, majestic, cross, and gray,
With red paint on my nose, or wear,
  Down in my grave till Judgment Day,
The ring of Essex burning there,
          If I were a Queen?

Now let me ask myself awhile.
  Mary of Scotland, then?—since she
Haunts her gray castle with a smile
  That one man may have died to see:
She, fairest in Romance's light;
  She, saddest-storied of them all;
She—but it would not please me quite
  To climb a scaffold, or to fall

Beside my lovely head to-night,
If I were a Queen.

Then she of Egypt—with the asp
To drain my deadly beauty dry?—
To see my Roman lover clasp
His sword with surer love, and die
Closer to it than me? Not so.
No desert-snake with nursing grace
Should draw my fierce heart's fiercest glow;
No coward of my conqueror's race
Should offer me his blood, I know—
If I were a Queen.

Boädicéa? I were afraid
To see her scythéd chariots shine!

——— Nor Vashti; for she disobeyed
  Her lord, the king in kingly wine!
Then she, the Queen of the East, who found
  The Wisest not so well arrayed,
In all his glory, as the ground
  Arrays its lilies?—Would I fade
Into some shrunken Bible mound,
                    If I were a Queen?

Semiramis? Were it not sweet
  To have a palace mirror show*
How mad Assyria at my feet
  Might lie down like a lamb? And, oh!
To stand defiant, in the glare
  Of rising war, and softly say:

* Allusion to a celebrated painting of Semiramis.

"My Beauty will subdue them!" Rare
  And royal bloom must drop away;
Nor would I as a ghost look fair,
          If I were a Queen.

Penelopé? No, on my word:
  Vexed grievously with suitors, while
Much-wandering Ulysses heard
  Fine singing at the syrens' isle,
Too small were Ithaca for me!
  Then she whose gold hair glitters high
With stars caught in its tangles?*—See,
  How beautiful it is! But I
Should choose my hair on Earth to be,
          If I were a Queen!

* Berenice's Hair.

Nor slight, blonde Marie Antoinette?
  Nor she the Austrians called their King?
Nor any Blanche, or Margaret?
  Nor Russia's Catharine? Would I bring
The Spanish woman's loath heart, then,
  From Aragon to England's throne?
Or be the Italian, widowed, when
  She, in a garret at Cologne,
Starved, a gray exile, shunned of men,
          If I were a Queen?

What Queen? Titania—since it seems
  A woman never quite can tire
Of kissing long, fair ears! In dreams
  My Gentle Joy I will admire,

And—but there is no Fairyland
  Left in the crowded world, no room
For dew, for any thing but sand.
  Put out the moonshine, fold the bloom.
My feet could find no space to stand,
        If I were a Queen.

Ah! still I ask myself what Queen?
  Well, one whose days were almost done,
Who felt her grave-grass turning green,
  Who saw the low light of the sun
Shrink from her palace windows, while
  Her whole court watched beside her bed,
Ready to say, without a smile:
"We loved the Queen. The Queen is dead."

Then they should grieve a little while,
If I were a Queen.

And my whole court, I think, should show
Three little heads of lightest gold,
Two others of a darker glow;
And One bent low enough to hold
Between pale, quivering hands. And then
Some Silence should receive my soul,
My name should fade from lips of men,
My pleasant funeral-bells should toll
This hour, and dust be dust again—
If I were a Queen.

THEIR TWO FORTUNES.

[*Annie, after calling on Charlotte.*]

"AS I passed her window she smiled at me,
Through the lovely mist of her laces,
And asked if I would go in and see
Those exquisite foreign vases.

"Then the mirrors here, or the bronzes there,
Or some statue's cold completeness,
Or the flowers that followed her through the air,
With their souls expressed in sweetness.

"From the carpets, full of their Eastern blooms,
That were hiding her steps so lightly,
I passed to the love in my faded rooms,
And my heart kept aching—slightly.

"If her life is dry, then its torrid sands
Must have pained my eyes with their glitter,
For I know that I hid my face in my hands—
And I fear that my tears were bitter.

"Ah, you pity her—because she is fair;
And because—she wears rich dresses;
And because her lord has—not dark hair;
And because of—certain guesses.

"But I tell you, sir, with your author's look,
  When the point of your pen grows tender
There are things as sad to put in your book
  As my lady's loveless splendor."

SOMETIME.

WELL, either you or I,
After whatever is to say is said,
Must see the other die,
Or hear, through distance, of the other dead,
Sometime.

And you or I must hide
Poor empty eyes and faces, wan and wet
With Life's great grief, beside
The other's coffin, sealed with silence, yet,
Sometime.

And you or I must look
  Into the other's grave, or far or near,
And read, as in a book
  Writ in the dust, words we made bitter here,
                    Sometime.

Then, through what paths of dew,
  What flush of flowers, what glory in the grass,
Only one of us two,
  Even as a shadow walking, blind may pass,
                    Sometime!

And, if the nestling song
  Break from the bosom of the bird for love,

No more to listen long
  One shall be deaf below, one deaf above,
          Sometime.

For both must lose the way
  Wherein we walk together, very soon:
One in the dusk shall stay,
  The other first shall see the rising moon,
          Sometime.

Oh! fast, fast friend of mine!
  Lift up the voice I love so much, and warn;
To wring faint hands and pine,
  Tell me I may be left forlorn, forlorn,
          Sometime.

Say I may kiss through tears,
  Forever falling and forever cold,
One ribbon from sweet years,
  One dear dead leaf, one precious ring of gold,
            Sometime.

Say you may think with pain
  Of some slight grace, some timid wish to please,
Some eager look half vain
  Into your heart, some broken sobs like these,
            Sometime!

THE DEAD FAIRIES.

"DO the Fairies ever die?"
Why, yes, they are always dying.
There in the freezing dark, close by,
A thousand, dead, are lying.

Of the time they made so fair
But the fading shadow lingers—
Oh, how the light gold of my hair
Curled on their airy fingers!

I shall not see them again:
  They fell in the sun's fierce brightening;
They were drowned in drops of——"Rain?"
  They were scorched to death with lightning.

With bloom, as the bee-songs pass,
  Our sweet-briar keeps its promise;
The fireflies burn in the grass;
  Winds blow our butterflies from us.

Yet, under that thin gray tree
  With the moonrise in its stillness,
They keep hidden away from me,
  Forever, in dusty chillness.

THE ORDER FOR HER PORTRAIT.

"I SAY what Cromwell said,
(Smile, gray-haired skeptic, if you think me bold,)
And that Italian count whose hair was red—
His great will would not have it painted gold.

"Look at me, if you will;
Say youth is gone, or youth was never mine.
I change not with the seasons. Cold and still,
I wait before you—careless and divine.

"Youth? Can the rose outstay
The bud of the rose? And could the round moon shine
Without the crescent somewhere? Who shall say
How far youth reaches? Not such voice is mine.

"No, I am brave, not vain;
Braver than he of Macedon, since I
For Vanity's light sake would hardly stain
Art and the awful future with a lie:

"You know that hand whose pride
Within its hollow held one world, afar
Reaching for others, raised itself to hide
On pictured brows the glory of a scar.

"But paint me as I am,
  Whatever shape or color you may see;
And do not fold the white fleece of the lamb
  About the yellow lioness, for me.

"Aye, as I am. And then,
  No matter what you on your canvas find,
It shall not shrink before the eyes of men;
  It shall be Truth—unless your soul is blind!"

"I WANT IT YESTERDAY."

"COME, take the flower, — it is not dead,
It stayed all night out in the dew."
"I will not have it now," he said;
"I want it yesterday, I do."

"It is as red, it is as sweet" ——
With angry tears he turned away,
Then flung it fiercely at his feet,
And said, "I want it — yesterday."

As sullen and as quick of grief,
  Sometimes a lovelier flower than this
I crush forever, scent and leaf;
  Then scent and leaf forever miss.

It keeps its blush, it keeps its breath,
  It keeps its form unchanged, but I
See in its beauty only death;
  Then drop it in the dust, — and why?

And why? Ah, Hand divine, I know, —
  Forgive my childish pain, I pray, —
To-day your flower is fair, but oh!
  I only want it — yesterday!

MARBLE OR DUST?

A CHILD, beside a statue, said to me,
With pretty wisdom very sadly just,
"That man is Mr. Lincoln, mamma. He
Was made of marble; we are made of dust."

One flash of passionate sorrow trembled through
The dust of which I had been dimly made,
One fierce, quick wish to be of marble too—
Not something meaner, that must fall and fade.

"To be forever fair and still and cold,"
  I faintly thought, with faint tears in my sight;
"To stand thus face to face with Time, and hold
  Between us that uncrumbling charm of white;

"To see the creatures formed of slighter stuff
  Waver in little dead-leaf whirls away,
Yet know that I could wait and have enough
  Of frost and dew, enough of dark and day.

"——— I would be marble? Wherefore? Just tc miss
  The tremors of glad pain that dust must know?—
The grief that settles after some dead kiss?—
  The frown that was a smile not long ago?

"Do I forget the stone's long loneliness?—
The dumb impatience all wan watching brings?—
The looking with blind eyes, in vague distress,
For Christ's slow Coming and the End of Things?

"No, boy of mine, with your young yellow hair,
Better the dust you scatter with your feet
Than marble, which can see not you are fair—
Than marble, which can feel not you are sweet.

"Ay, or than marble which must meet the years
Without my light relief of murmurous breath;
Without the bitter sweetness of my tears—
Without the love which dust must have for Death."

THEIR LOST PICTURE.

"NO, it was nothing old and grand:
Only a child, out in the sun,
Choking a kitten with one hand,
And crushing pretty flowers with one.

"Some rose-buds, sweet as buds could be,
Were blown against the blowing hair;
The clear eyes watched a cedar-tree,
That held a red-bird flaming there.

"The frame around was dark and small.
Just opposite the open door,
One morning, on our cottage wall
It hung, when we were young and poor.

"This little piece of light and bloom
Was more, a thousand times, to me
Than all you have seen in great church-gloom,
Or palace-gallery light, could be.

"——— You do not understand, I say.
We saw the picture in the glass,
In our first home so far away,
When our dead child played in the grass."

SEEING THROUGH TEARS.

AH me! look not too fair!
If Love could be a fairy story, ending
At our two graves out in the dark somewhere—
If, dying, I could know myself descending
Forever from myself, no cry
For wings would smite the sky;

No high reproach and fond
That souls and angels were frail human fancies

That nothing, sweet or bitter, was beyond
  The Bible saints and their divine romances:—
      All I could feel were this, I fear—
      That dust to dust is dear!

TO-MORROW.

KEEP lovely in that painted scene,
 There where false water quivers bright,
There where false-fruited trees are green,
 Far from the sharp Dawn's dreary light,
 Our dear Illusion of To-night!

Only with lamps between we meet,
 With silence in your steps you stay:
A Player, seeming young and sweet,

That have to play a bitter play—
Near, yet forever far away.

You, in your borrowed hair's fair gloom;
You, in your mask of white and red;
You, in mock jewels—bud and bloom,
Torn from To-day, with odors dead,
Will stain the shining stage you tread!

We tremble as we feel you start,
So dimly glittering toward our eyes,
For this dark drama, this fierce part,
Where coffins, blood, and tearful cries
Must pass you in your pageantries.

Ah! lovely in that painted scene,
There where false water quivers bright,
There where false-fruited trees are green,
Far from the sharp Dawn's dreary light,
Stay, dear Illusion of To-night!

SWEETNESS OF BITTERNESS.

I WONDER, if my hair were gray,
It would not then be sweet to see
Some other head in gold, and say,
Shaking my own: "Ah me! ah me!
How very pleasant it must be
To have such lovely hair as she!"

I wonder, if my days were shut,
Empty and dim and slow with care,
In some poor peasant's prison-hut,
It would not then be sweet to stare,
With the fierce boldness of despair,
Into some shining window, where

Each foreign flower, through lifted lace,
  Its passionate, homesick yearning shows,
On pictures warm with Southern grace
  Or cold with Northern birds and snows,
  And say: "How fair a fate have those
  Within whose world such beauty glows."

I wonder, if the broken breath
  Of one wet brier-rose held to-night
A little memory dear with death,
  It were not sweet to have the light
  Show laughing mothers full in sight
  Kiss dimpled things in baby-white.

I wonder, were I left alone,
  With asp and sun and sand, some day,
And circled with a fiery zone,

'T would not be sweet to look away
Toward lands where moonlit fountains play
And toss to other lips their spray.

I wonder, were it mine to kiss
A nun's black cross through tears, and wear
Her blinding veil, and miss and miss
The world's one charm, if even there,
High up in still and sacred air,
Where thought itself is only prayer,

It would not then be sweet to make
(And like a mateless bird to pine)
My wan and weary fingers ache
With tracing some light leaf or vine
In bridal drapery, faint and fine—
Because it never could be mine!

I wonder, is there any thing
  In hidden honey half so sweet
As—something in the bee's wild sting;
  If buried wine, found at the feet
  Of some young king, were so complete
  As thirst within his fever's heat.

A WOMAN'S ANSWER.

[*After Many Years.*]

THE king a story is to-day—
You know the story vague and splendid?
His name is withered, dim, and gray;
His deeds are ruins in the play
Of ghostly lightning, sometime seen
On lonesome heights, where, fair and green,
The dewy legend clings around;
Yet, by his Paladins attended,

Through Romance once his horn was wound,
And listening lands shook with the sound.

In this brief world a little time
  To be a king this king was fated;
But how imperial and sublime
His after-palace was! No rhyme
Can hold its quiet or its gloom:
Three hundred years within a tomb,
Before his awful reign was done,
  Three hundred years and more he waited,
Fixed on his marble throne, where none
Could bring him news of star or sun.

He sat, a skeleton, beside
  The glare of gold; and many a jewel

Blazed fiercely from its shrine to hide
The nothingness of death with pride.
Crown, sword, and scepter world-adored,
Dead crown, dead scepter, and dead sword
Upheld thus by a dead right arm,
  The glory of the grave is cruel!
His regal mantle was not warm,
Nor did his queen's ring keep its charm.

Oh, after that last battle, peace
  To him and all his heroes, shining
So long in lovely raiment. . . . Cease,
Poor, murmurous heart of mine! . . . His lease
Of royal centuries slowly fled—
A living king dethroned the dead,

Spite of the True Cross on his breast,
  With faith for ages round it twining:
For God at last said it was best
To give the patient emperor rest.

My king, you reigned in flowering air,
  In my light life, not long. My fancies,
Your Paladins, were brave and fair,
And followed you with loyal care
To—Font Arabia? And, at last,
Fallen and scarred and worn, they passed
Into some shadow, where they lie
  With red stains on their weary lances;
And some slow death that can not die
Broods low between them and the sky.

Three hundred years and more to me,
  You, like the medieval giant,
In fixed and fearful majesty
Down in a sepulcher could be,
And glitter with a ghostly state;
But some strange king came, slow and late,
To lift your throne above the ground,
  And sit thereon with bloom defiant—
Spite of the True Cross with you found—
After his shining head was crowned.

THE FAVORITE CHILD.

WHICH of five snowdrops would the moon
Think whitest, if the moon could see?
Which of five rosebuds flushed with June
Were reddest to the mother-tree?
Which of five birds, that play one tune
On their soft-shining throats, may be
Chief singer? Who will answer me?

Would not the moon know, if around
One snowdrop any shadow lay?—

Would not the rose-tree, if the ground
  Should let one blossom droop a day?
Does not the one bird take a sound
  Into the cloud, when caught away,
  Finer than all the sounds that stay?

Oh, little, quiet boy of mine,
  Whose yellow head lies languid here—
Poor yellow head, its restless shine
  Brightened the butterflies last year!—
Whose pretty hands may intertwine
  With paler hands unseen but near:
  You are my favorite now, I fear!

THE CLOTHES OF A GHOST.

[*The Spirit of a Beautiful and Vain Woman speaks.*]

THEY were shut from me in a costly chest,
Though I, in a woman's slight, sad way,
Of the lovely things that I loved the best,
Held none, I fear me, so sweet as they—
For I was daintily dressed!

A precious glimmer of gold was mine,
To coil and charm on my bosom then;

And two great jewels whose restless shine
Troubled the foolish hearts of men,
Who fancied their light divine.

These thin hands wore on their tremulous grace
Such fair little gloves as soft as snows;
And softly laid on this dim, fixed face
Were calm, clear colors of white and rose,
In another time and place.

There's a withering, weird half-picture of Me—
No, of my Clothes—on a shadowy wall:
A wonderful painter, they said, was he,
Who studied my drapery, that was all,
Not guessing what I might be.

Yet he followed me, in my far, flushed day,
  And thought he knew me, and held me dear;
And now, should I waver across his way,
  He would grow as ghastly as I am, with fear,
      Though he is so wise and gray!

But my beautiful Clothes were his despair—
  They were so well-cut, so charmingly made.
It is best that they were not worn threadbare;
  It is best that I did not feel them fade;
      It is best—did *he* ever care?

I, a Thing too fearfully fine to show,
  Or stain the starlight wherein I pass,
Must still have the old, fierce vanity grow,

Must yearn by the water, as by a glass,
For a glimpse of—Nothing, I know!

Oh, my lovely Clothes that I still admire!
They were only fashioned for moth and rust;
Yet I, their Wearer, though scarred by fire,
Shall sit with the gentle ghosts, I trust,
Who once wore meaner attire!

For, had I been less like the lilies arrayed—
They of the field that toil not nor spin—
I had thought of my Father's work, nor stayed
In empty glory, in shining sin,
Far into the final shade.

FLIGHT.

THROUGH field and flood and fire I go,—
Wherefore and where I do not know.

Through field,—my tangled path is crossed
With winds and stinging spears of frost.

Through field,—the stones rise up and wound
My fearful feet, that stain the ground.

Through field, — sometimes one rose forlorn
Gives me its flush, without its thorn.

Through flood, — the wide rains beat my brow;
The world is only water now.

Through flood, — wave after wave there is:
Wave after wave, — what else but this?

Through flood, — one sea another meets;
See Arctic ice in tropic heats!

Through flood, — there is one ship in sight:
If I might reach it, — if I might!

Through fire, — what flames and flames there be!
The world is only fire to me.

Through fire, — how palace spire and wall
Put shining garments on and fall!

Through fire, — I hear the last voice cry,
"The world is ashes." But am I?

Calm on the awful element,
I turn and say, "I am content."

BEATRICE CENCI.

[*Seen in a City Shop-window.*]

OUT of low light an exquisite faint face
Suddenly started. Goldenness of hair,
A South-look of sweet-sorrowful eyes, a trace
Of prison-paleness: what if these were there,
When Guido's hand could never reach the grace
That glimmered on me from the Italian air—
Fairness so fierce, or fierceness half so fair?

"Is it some Actress?" a slight school-boy said.
Some Actress? Yes.
——The curtain rolled away,
Dusty and dim. The scene—among the dead—
In some weird, gloomy-pillared palace lay;
The Tragedy, which we have brokenly read,
With its two hundred ghastly years was gray:
None dared applaud with flowers her shadowy way—
Yet, ah! how bitterly well she seemed to play!

Hush! for a child's quick murmur breaks the charm
Of terror that was winding round me so;
And, at the white touch of her pretty arm,
Darkness and Death and Agony crouch low

In old-time dungeons: "Tell me, (is it harm
To ask you?) *is* the picture real, though?—
And why the beautiful ladies, all, you know,
Live so far-off, and die so long ago?"

OVER IN KENTUCKY.

"THIS is the smokiest city in the world,"
A slight voice, wise and weary, said, "I know.
My sash is tied, and, if my hair was curled,
I'd like to have my prettiest hat and go
There where some violets had to stay, you said,
Before your torn-up butterflies were dead—
Over in Kentucky."

Then one, whose half-sad face still wore the hue
The North Star loved to light and linger on,

Before the war, looked slowly at me too,
  And darkly whispered: "What is gone is gone.
Yet, though it may be better to be free,
I'd rather have things as they used to be
          Over in Kentucky."

Perhaps I thought how fierce the master's hold,
  Spite of all armies, kept the slave within;
How iron chains, when broken, turned to gold,
  In empty cabins, where glad songs had been
Before the Southern sword knew blood and rust,
Before wild cavalry sprang from the dust,
          Over in Kentucky.

Perhaps———but, since two eyes, half-full of tears,
  Half-full of sleep, would love to keep awake

With fairy pictures from my fairy years,
  I have a phantom pencil that can make
Shadows of moons, far back and faint, to rise
On dewier grass and in diviner skies,
                    Over in Kentucky.

For yonder river, wider than the sea,
  Seems sometimes in the dusk a visible moan
Between two worlds—one fair, one dear to me.
  The fair has forms of ever-glimmering stone,
Weird-whispering ruin, graves where legends hide,
And lies in mist upon the charmèd side,
                    Over in Kentucky.

The dear has restless, dimpled, pretty hands,
  Yearning toward unshaped steel, unfancied wars,

Unbuilded cities, and unbroken lands,
  With something sweeter than the faded stars
And dim, dead dews of my lost romance, found
In beauty that has vanished from the ground
          Over in Kentucky.

CINCINNATI, *Ohio.*

AN EAST INDIAN FAIRY STORY.

ALL day she was yellow and gray and thin;
All day she was troubled with time and tears;
All day she was dressed in the withered skin
Of a woman who lived a hundred years.

All day she begged, through the heavy heat,
For a drop of water, a grain of rice;
But she sat, in the twilight, still and sweet,
Close to the leaves of the blossoming spice.

At a fairy fountain dim in the air,
In a garment white as a priestess wears,
With a lotus-bud in her lovely hair,
And her hand in the water, she said her prayers.

"Oh, well do I hide my beauty all day
From the sun and the cruel eyes I dread;
But the gods can see me when I pray,
And I must look fair to the gods," she said.

BABY OR BIRD?

"BUT is he a Baby or a Bird?"
Sometimes I fancy I do not know;
His voice is as sweet as I ever heard
Far up where the light leaves blow.

Then his lovely eyes, I think, would see
As clear as a Bird's in the upper air;
And his red-brown head, it seems to me,
Would do for a Bird to bear.

"If he were a Bird," you wisely say,
  "He would have some wings to know him by:"
Ah, he has wings, that are flying away
  Forever—how fast they fly!

They are flying with him, by day, by night;
  Under suns and stars, over storm and snow,
These fair, fine wings, that elude the sight,
  In softest silence they go.

Come, kiss him as often as you may———
  Hush, never talk of this time next year,
For the same small Bird that we pet to-day,
  To-morrow is never here!

SAY THE SWEET WORDS.

SAY the sweet words, say them soon;
You have said the bitter—
Changed to tears, by this dim moon
You may see them glitter.

Say the sweet words soon, I pray—
Mine is piteous pleading:
Haste to draw the steel away,
Though the wound keep bleeding.

A BUTTERFLY'S MESSAGE.

OUT in the dark, imploring hands I wrung,
And reached for pity yearningly and high,
While my own soul, with fierce fever stung,
Answered him, cry for cry——
"Come in, and see him die."

Come in and see him die? That was not he
So white and strange, so like the very dead.
Far back in dew and flowers could I not see
His pretty glimmering head,
And torn straw hat, instead?

I moaned and moaned: "Oh, give me back my
 child!"
An Angel laid a small white garment by,
And looked at me through tears. I only smiled,
To see him fly and fly
Alone through God's fair sky.

"I will be very patient now and sweet,"
I whispered to the Angel as he flew,
"And lead—through thorns, it must be—little feet
Forever nearer you."
But—what I was he knew!

"If I forget, send me some silent sign—
That butterfly he used to follow so,
Or its next summer-ghost, shall seem divine

Reproof, and I shall know.
Oh! hear me as you go."

To-day, when some small want had made me fret,
A sudden butterfly wavered around.
Blown from another world it was, and yet
I felt a subtle wound.
It would not touch the ground.

The passionate words, "Give back my child," the vow
To the still Angel which last year I made,
And broke, were bitterly remembered now;
And I was sore afraid
There in the haunted shade.

Because no phantom child is following you,
  Come to me often, phantom butterfly!
Help me to keep my tearful promise true;
  For when you tremble by,
  My guilty heart knows why.

LEAVING LOVE.

"IF one should stay in Italy a while,
With bloom to hide the dust beneath her feet,
With birds in love with roses to beguile
Her life until its sadness grew too sweet;

"If she should, slowly, see some statue there,
Divine with whiteness and with coldness, keep
A very halo in the hovering air;
If she should weep—because it could not weep;

"If she should waste each early gift of grace
In watching it with rapturous despair,
Should kiss her youth out on its stony face,
And feel the grayness gathering toward her hair:

"Then fancy, though it had till now seemed blind,
Blind to her little fairness, it could see
How scarred of soul, how wan and worn of mind,
How faint of form and faded, she must be;

"If she should moan: 'Ah, land of flower and fruit,
Ah, fiercely languid land, undo your charm!
Ah, song impassioned, make your music mute!
Ah, bosom, shake away my clinging arm!'

"Then swiftly climb into the mountains near,
And set her face forever toward the snow,
And feel the North in chasm and cliff, and hear
No echo from the fairyland below;

"If she should feel her own new loneliness,
With every deep-marked, freezing step she trod,
Nearing (and in its nearness growing less)
The vast and utter loneliness of God;

"If back to scented valleys she should call,
This woman that I fancy—only she—
Would it remind one statue there at all,
O cruel Silence in the South, of—me?"

THE BLACK PRINCESS.

[*A true Fable of my old Kentucky Nurse.*]

I KNEW a Princess: she was old,
Crisp-haired, flat-featured, with a look
Such as no dainty pen of gold
Would write of in a Fairy Book.

So bent she almost crouched, her face
Was like the Sphinx's face, to me,
Touched with vast patience, desert grace,
And lonesome, brooding mystery.

What wonder that a faith so strong
  As hers, so sorrowful, so still,
Should watch in bitter sands so long,
  Obedient to a burdening will!

This Princess was a Slave—like one
  I read of in a painted tale;
Yet free enough to see the sun,
  And all the flowers, without a vail.

Not of the Lamp, not of the Ring,
  The helpless, powerful Slave was she,
But of a subtler, fiercer Thing:
  She was the Slave of Slavery.

Court-lace nor jewels had she seen:
  She wore a precious smile, so rare
That at her side the whitest queen
  Were dark—her darkness was so fair.

Nothing of loveliest loveliness
  This strange, sad Princess seemed to lack;
Majestic with her calm distress
  She was, and beautiful though black:

Black, but enchanted black, and shut
  In some vague Giant's tower of air,
Built higher than her hope was. But
  The True Knight came and found her there.

The Knight of the Pale Horse, he laid
His shadowy lance against the spell
That hid her Self: as if afraid,
The cruel blackness shrank and fell.

Then, lifting slow her pleasant sleep,
He took her with him through the night,
And swam a River cold and deep,
And vanished up an awful Height.

And, in her Father's House beyond,
They gave her beauty robe and crown:
——On me, I think, far, faint, and fond,
Her eyes to-day look, yearning, down.

ONE POET'S SILENCE.

THROUGH all his youth he heard the Greek
winds blow—
The very voices of the Muses they,
Speaking, mysterious and ghostly-low,
Out of the dusk, two thousand years away.

He saw Olympus in its ancient glow:
But then he saw light foreign children play,
In some great temple roofed with heaven, below,
With waxen dolls in dresses thin and gay.

He looked at them and murmured: "Even so
  Do all the little poets of to-day
Set their poor painted images for show
  In temples where the gods alone should stay."

HER SIMILE.

"IF you should see a statue, one
Whose marble name was Silence, sit alone,
Whiter than Death and sadder, in the sun,
With stony finger pressed to lips of stone;

"If from those lips, themselves so still,
A fountain's waters restlessly should start,
And make a little troubled murmur, till
They all were dry: this would be like my heart."

A PRETTIER BOOK.

"HE has a prettier book than this,"
With many a sob between, he said;
Then left untouched the night's last kiss,
And, sweet with sorrow, went to bed.

A prettier book his brother had?—
Yet wonder-pictures were in each.
The different colors made him sad;
The equal value — could I teach?

Ah, who is wiser? . . . Here we sit,
  Around the world's great hearth, and look,
While Life's fire-shadows flash and flit,
  Each wistful in another's book.

I see, through fierce and feverish tears,
  Only a darkened hut in mine;
Yet in my brother's book appears
  A palace where the torches shine.

A peasant, seeking bitter bread
  From the unwilling earth to wring,
Is in my book; the wine is red,
  There in my brother's, for the king.

A wedding, where each wedding-guest
  Has wedding garments on, in his, —
In mine one face in awful rest,
  One coffin never shut, there is!

In his, on many a bridge of beams
  Between the faint moon and the grass,
Dressed daintily in dews and dreams,
  The fleet midsummer fairies pass;

In mine unearthly mountains rise,
  Unearthly waters foam and roll,
And — stared at by its deathless eyes —
  The master sells the fiend a soul!

. . . Put out the lights. We will not look
At pictures any more. We weep,
"My brother has a prettier book,"
And, after tears, we go to sleep.

"A PRECIOUS SEEING."

MY fairies, weary of snow and fire,
  Of frost on window and ice on tree,
I can show you Summer until you tire;
  Come—look behind you awhile and see:
Why, here is the nest in our old bent brier,
  Where the brown bird used to be!

Ah, here is the brown bird, just as shy,
  In the little leaves, with her warm wings down

On the wee white eggs, that, bye and bye,
  Will change into other birds as brown——
If you go too near you will make her fly,
  And that may make me frown.

And here is the flower you must not touch—
  The first that bloomed in our grass, you know.
Your butterflies, look!—were there ever such?—
  Wild with the sun they glitter and go.
And here are the lambs you loved so much—
  How little they seem to grow!

And here are the berries black and sweet;
  And here, in the glimmer of lightning-flies,

Is the gray strange man you used to meet,
  Who walked at evening—to reach the skies?
Oh, never look up through the dark and sleet—
  Look down in your own fair eyes!

THE FUNERAL OF A DOLL.

THEY used to call her Little Nell,
In memory of that lovely child
Whose story each had learned to tell.
She, too, was slight and still and mild,
Blue-eyed and sweet; she always smiled,
And never troubled any one
Until her pretty life was done.
And so they tolled a tiny bell,
That made a wailing fine and faint,

As fairies ring, and all was well.
  Then she became a waxen saint.

Her funeral it was small and sad.
  Some birds sang bird-hymns in the air.
The humming-bee seemed hardly glad,
  Spite of the honey every-where.
  The very sunshine seem'd to wear
Some thought of death, caught in its gold,
That made it waver wan and cold.
Then, with what broken voice he had,
  The Preacher slowly murmured on
(With many warnings to the bad)
  The virtues of the Doll now gone.

A paper coffin rosily-lined
Had Little Nell. There, drest in white,
With buds about her, she reclined,
A very fair and piteous sight—
Enough to make one sorry, quite.
And, when at last the lid was shut
Under white flowers, I fancied ——— but
No matter. When I heard the wind
Scatter Spring-rain that night across
The Doll's wee grave, with tears half-blind
One child's heart felt a grievous loss.

"It was a funeral, mamma. Oh,
Poor Little Nell is dead, is dead.

How dark!—and do you hear it blow?
  She is afraid." And, and as she said
  These sobbing words, she laid her head
Between her hands and whispered: "Here
Her bed is made, the precious dear—
She can not sleep in it, I know.
  And there is no one left to wear
Her pretty clothes. *Where did she go?*
  ———See, this poor ribbon tied her hair!"

A PARTING GIFT OF YOUTH.

AT the last dusk of May we stood together,
In the weird waning of the last Spring moon,
Too blind with tears for either to see whether
The other thought: "To-morrow will be June."

His name was Youth. I saw the rose-bud, flushing
His wet cheek, fade into the full rose there;
The music at his lip crept toward a hushing,
And all the light gold darken'd in his hair.

I knew his beauty had grown fainter, finer;
 I knew the time was come for him to go.
Yet never had his presence seemed diviner,
 And never, never did I love him so.

He held a cold hand toward me with a tremor:
 I dropped it, and he turned away his head.
"Good bye—good bye. I was a pretty dreamer,
 Yet you will not regret me much," he said.

"I have a Gift to leave with you, at leaving—
 Worth more perhaps than I could ever be.
Keep it forever, and—forget your grieving.
 A woman has no time to grieve for me."

"So he will go," I thought. "Ah well, he fancies
I scarce am young enough to please him now.
The Fairy Books are read; and light romances,
Perhaps, are rather tiresome anyhow.

"What precious keepsake will you leave, my lover?—
A statue for a niche in some rich room,
Where light with costly stains is drifted over
Fair laces and great jewel-wreaths in bloom?"

Ah, Youth had vanished from me like a vision.
A statue for a niche? Such choice was mine.
He left instead, in beautiful derision,
For cottage windows, just one climbing vine.

And, year by year, the young buds gather sweetly;
  And, year by year, I wear them in my breast,
Knowing but this: that, wisely and completely,
  My lovely Giver knew which Gift was best.

CRYING FOR THE MOON.

IT is very pretty because it is high;
All things are pretty when out of reach,
And the prettiest things are kept in the sky.
Why? Can I ever tell you why?
God, I think, knows better than I.
I shall have to learn what I can not teach.

But it is yellow sometimes, do you say,
And sometimes red?—and you want it, too?
I wonder how long it would please your play.

Remember it does not shine by day,
And at night you'd have to put it away—
  You could not take it to bed with you.

Yes, but you can not have it, I fear—
  For a reason as good as we find in books:
For people as wise as you, and as queer,
Will cry for the moon, year after year,
And go to their graves without it, my dear:
  Because—it is larger than it looks!

AUNT ANNIE.

THE old house has, for being sweet,
Some sweeter reason than the rose
Which, red or white, about the feet
Of many a nested home-bird grows.

And sadder reason than the rain
On the quaint porch, for being sad,
(Oh, human pity, human pain!)
The old house, in its shadows, had.

I sat within it as a guest,
  I who went from it as a wife;—
The young days there, though not the best,
  Had been the fairest of my life:

For love itself must ever seem
  More precious, to our restless youth,
When hovering subtly in its dream
  Than when we touch its nestling truth.

I sat there as a guest, I said—
  Holding the loveliest boy on earth,
With his fair, sleepy, yellow head
  Close to the pleasant shining hearth.

He laughed out in his sleep, and I
  Laughed too, and kissed him—when I heard
A wise and very cautious sigh;
  And once again the dimples stirred.

Aunt Annie looked at him awhile;
  Then shook her head at her own fears,
With more of sorrow in her smile
  Than I could ever put in tears.

"He *is* a pretty boy I know—
  The prettiest in the world? Ah, me!
One other, fifty years ago,
  Was quite as pretty, dear, as he.

"Now I am eighty. Twenty-five
Are gone since last we heard from James.
I sometimes think he is alive."
She hushed, and looked into the flames.

"He used to tell me, when a child,
Of far, strange countries, where they say
The flowers bloom all the year"—she smiled—
"I can't believe it, to this day!

"And still I think he may have crossed
The sea—and stayed the other side.
His letters may have all been lost—
Who knows? Who knows? The world is wide.

"I often think, if you could know
  How much he makes me think of *him*,
You 'd guess why I love Victor so."
  Again the troubled eyes were dim.

"If your child, such a night, were out
  Lost in this dark and snow and sleet,
You would go wild, I do not doubt."
  I almost heard her own heart beat.

"Yet long, on stormier nights than this,
  Mine has been out—why should I care
How many a winter now it is?
  Mine has been out—and God knows where."

THE PALACE-BURNER.

A PICTURE IN A NEWSPAPER.

SHE has been burning palaces. "To see
The sparks look pretty in the wind?" Well, yes—
And something more. But women brave as she
Leave much for cowards, such as I, to guess.

But this is old, so old that everything
Is ashes here—the woman and the rest.
Two years are—oh! so long. Now you may bring
Some newer pictures. You like this one best?

You wish that you had lived in Paris then?—
  You would have loved to burn a palace, too?
But they had guns in France, and Christian men
  Shot wicked little Communists like you.

You would have burned the palace?—Just because
  You did not live in it yourself! Oh! why
Have I not taught you to respect the laws?
  You would have burned the palace—would not *I?*

Would I? Go to your play. Would I, indeed?
  I? Does the boy not know my soul to be
Languid and worldly, with a dainty need
  For light and music? Yet he questions me.

Can he have seen my soul more near than I?
  Ah! in the dusk and distance sweet she seems,
With lips to kiss away a baby's cry,
  Hands fit for flowers, and eyes for tears and dreams.

Can he have seen my soul? And could she wear
  Such utter life upon a dying face:
Such unappealing, beautiful despair:
  Such garments—soon to be a shroud—with grace?

Has she a charm so calm that it could breathe
  In damp, low places till some frightened hour;
Then start, like a fair, subtle snake, and wreathe
  A stinging poison with a shadowy power?

Would *I* burn palaces? The child has seen
In this fierce creature of the Commune here,
So bright with bitterness and so serene,
A being finer than my soul, I fear.

LOVE-STORIES.

CAN I tell any? No:
I have forgotten all I ever knew.
I am too old. I saw the fairies go
Forever from the moonshine and the dew
Before I met with you.

"Rose's grandmother knows
Love-stories?" *She* could tell you one or two?

"*She* is not young?" You wish that you were
Rose?
"*She* hears love-stories? Are they ever true?"
Some time I may ask you.

I was not living when
Columbus came here, nor before that? So
You wonder when I saw the fairies, then?
The Indians would have killed them all, you
know?
"How *long* is long ago?"

And if I am too old
To know love-stories, why am I not good?

Why do n't I read the Bible, and not scold?
Why do n't I pray, as all old ladies should?
(I only wish I could.)

Why do n't I buy gray hair?
And why ———
Oh! child, the Sphinx herself might spring
Out of her sands to answer, should you dare
Her patience with your endless questioning.
"Does *she* know any thing?"

Perhaps. "Then, could she tell
Love-stories?" If her lips were not all stone;

For there is one she must remember well—
One whose great glitter showed a fiery zone
Brightness beyond its own.

One whose long music aches—
How sharp the sword, how sweet the snake, O Queen!—
Into the last unquiet heart that breaks.
But the Nile-lily rises faint betwen ———
You wonder what I mean?

I mean there is but one
Love-story in this withered world, forsooth;

And it is brief, and ends, where it begun,
(What if I tell, in play, the dreary truth?)
With something we call Youth.

HIS FAIRY GODMOTHER.

[CINDERELLA SPEAKS.]

WHO felt the quaint light subtly shining in?—
Who heard that other wind within the wind?
Who saw the Little Lady, wild and thin,
Pale with the spirits and the spells behind?

I see her now; I take this withered wand,
A weird Egyptian lily, when I choose,

And wave her to and fro, and back beyond
That lonesome moonshine and those charméd dews.

I see her now—if I but shut my eyes—
Dressed in the frosty green of leaves half-dead:
Ah, still witch-smile; ah, old and wise replies
To all the precious words—you never said!

How queer you both looked as she rose and shook
Her ancient, shrunken, clinched hand in your face,
Then laid her finger on your lip and took,
Beside you in the dance, her sudden place!

You play the Prince. Princes grow gray like you.
'Tis the worn story slightly changed, in truth:
Poor Cinderella never found her shoe;
She is left out—a fable of your youth.

You have the citrons and the wine of life,
Its lights, its honors—what has it beside?
Her Majesty, the Queen, your worthy wife,
Has plumes and pearls and garments purple-dyed.

She, in a peasant's cottage, built low down,
Kisses gold heads and waits a twilight voice,
Nor envies you the palace and the crown,
But finds her own in your godmother's choice.

Still she finds time, in dreaming, evermore,
 To wonder if, in flying sleep, you pass,
Handsome and young, sometimes, from your great
 door,
To kiss and keep—a Slipper made of Glass!

WHY SHOULD WE CARE?

WELL, if the bee should sting the flower to
death,
With just one drop of honey for the stinging;
If the high bird should break its airy breath,
And lose the song forever with the singing,
Why should we care?

If in our magic-books no charm is found
To call back last night's moon from last night's
distance;

If violets can not stay the whole year round,
  Spite of their odor and the dew's resistance,
      Why should we care?

If hands nor hearts like ours have strength to hold
  Fierce shining toys, nor treasures sweet and
      simple;
If nothing can be ours for love or gold;
  If kisses can not keep a baby's dimple,
      Why should we care?

If sand is in the South, frost in the North,
  And sorrow every-where, and passionate yearn-
      ing;

If stars fade from the skies; if men go forth
  From their own thresholds and make no returning,
    Why should we care?

If this same world can never be the same
  After this instant, but grows grayer, older,
And nearer to the silence whence it came;
  If faith itself is fainter, stiller, colder,
    Why should we care?

If the soft grass is but a pretty vail
  Spread on our graves to hide them when we
    enter;
And, after we are gone, if light should fail,

And fires should eat the green world to its
center,
Why should we care?

If tears were dry and laughter should seem strange;
And if the soul should doubt itself and falter:
Since God is God, and He can never change,
The fashions of the earth and Heaven may alter,
Why should we care?

AT THE PLAY.

I HAVE been to the play, my child.
  Night after night I go.
What if the weather be wild?—
  I am used to rain and snow.

Shakspeare's Poor Player is there.
  The stage is wide and dim.
The music is old, and rare
  Are the flowers I fling to him.

And the Play keeps wavering. But,
  Through forest and desert and sea,
By palace and temple and hut,
  The charm is the same to me.

The gods stand by in stone,
  With calm in their awful eyes;
Christ clings to his cross, alone
  In the bitter world, and dies.

The Player wears all the while,
  As soldier, or priest, or king,
Or peasant, the same sad smile;
  And the Play is—the same sad thing.

With jewels the boxes shine;
  Fierce eyes look out of the pit;
All whisper: "The Play is fine,"
  And all are weary of it.

But the Player is at his best
  In the shadow-scene—you shrink?—
Where he falls on his Brother's breast,
  (His Brother is Death,) I think.

"I WISH THAT I COULD GO."

THEY who look backward always look through
tears.
So, very dimly, somewhere, I do see
A door that opens into lonesome years,
Furnished with — dust and silence! What
can be
Sadder than absence of fair household sights,
Belovéd pictures, warm and pleasant lights,
In empty rooms where —— Does it call to me,

That first child-voice which taught my life to kno
What music meant?—
"I wish that I could go."

I turned and kissed her—"You had better stay
She heard the wood-bells ring among th
herds:
"I want to see so many lambs to-day,"
She answered in her little piteous words,
Sweetly half-said and tenderly half-guessed;
"You said there was one robin with a nest
Up in the apple-flowers. I love the birds—
Ever so many times—and you could show
Me where they sleep. I wish that I could go."

"It is too far. And here are butterflies;
Look—one—two—three. Go, catch them if
you will."
"I've seen all these too much—they hurt my eyes!
They're naughty things—they never can be
still!
I would not try to catch another one
Here, in the yard, to save its life! I'd run
After some pretty new ones on the hill
Away off—almost to the skies! And, oh!
I'd be so sweet. I wish that I could go."

Nor was it only toward the clear white light,
Led subtly on by many a violet,

She would have followed me. The great fierce Night
Might lie beside our cottage, black and wet,
And make mad hungry noises. Still, if I
Thought fit to pass it, her appealing cry
(The same that haunts me, sorrowfully, yet)
Was with me always—most forlorn and slow:
"If it *is* dark, I wish that I could go."

"If it is dark?"—what was the Dark? She knew
Just a brief bridge which others must have passed—
With a slight shiver, it might be—into
A glitter of lamps: a life whose heart beat fast

Under sweet colors, jewels, music, all
The showers of fairy gifts that, fairily, fall
  On some Strange City, where —— Oh! faint
    and vast,
Time lies behind, yet nearer seems to grow
That eager sound:
          "I wish that I could go."

It is in my own soul. Myself a child,
  Some ghostly doorway with my grief I fill;
Eager for blossoms beautiful and wild
  Just out of reach; eager to climb some hill,
So far away and almost to the skies,
And (tired of old ones) find new butterflies.

Some One seems gone whom I would follow
still.
Across the Dark I see your charméd glow,
Strange City, shine———
"I wish that I could go."

A LIFE IN A MIRROR.

O PRETTY Prisoner, young and sweet,
But just a little white and worn,
It makes my heart ache when I meet
Such beauty so forlorn;

To think the lilies in your grass
Must glimmer out and you not know,
That flocks of butterflies must pass
And still elude you so;

To think there is a sun by day,
  A moon whose fairness fills the night,
Yet you, a captive, pine—away
  From every lovely sight.

You babble much of foreign things:
  How you have seen the world, perchance;
And how great generals and kings
  Have asked you once to dance.

Your peerless face has made you dream!
  For in your life you never was
(Though far away you sometimes seem)
  Outside of your own glass.

In it you sleep, in it you wake,
  In it at last your dust shall be—
For Death, and only Death, can break
  Your fate and set you free!

WHEN the full moon's light is burning
At its brightest, it is pleasant,
Sometimes, blindly to sit yearning
For the slightness of the crescent;

When the finished rose is shining
In the sun with flushed completeness,
For the vanished bud repining,
Wilfully to miss its sweetness.

OUR OLD AND NEW LANDLORDS—1869 70.

"PERHAPS," One kindly said, through his
gray smile,
"I've been a generous Landlord, on the whole;
My tenants will remember me a while,
And pay for some sweet masses for my soul.

"They have had warm-dyed wool and linens fine;
My fair wide harvests gave them daily bread;
I sent them, for their weddings, fruits and wine,
And—flowers, too, for the coffins of their dead.

"For Travel I have done some handsome things;
The old East has her grand Canal at last,

Whose plan winds vaguely to her spice-sealed kings;
The West on her new Railway journeys fast.

"There has been trouble that I could not reach:
God pity this—to Him I leave the rest,
And Church and State——but I'll not make a speech!
For Church and State are bitter at the best.

"Now as for Spain and all her castles—well,
I've advertised her royal residence,
Which for good reasons was to let, or sell:
An Occupant will come—no matter whence.

"Then, Rome—why should I worry about Rome?
  The Holy Father is—infirm, I say,
And needs grave Council at St. Peter's dome,
  Where let him keep his Chamber while he may.

"Make ready now for greeting and good cheer—
  (And let your tears for me be few, at most);
Enjoy yourselves with this Young Fellow here,
  And pledge with laugh and song my worthy
      Ghost!"

The Other, springing boyish on the scene,
  Salutes with careless grace high Guests around;
Nods to the Emperor, the Sultan, the Queen,
  And makes our President a bow profound!

"Your Excellency, let 's have a cigar,
(His Majesty, there, can no longer smoke,)
And talk of—horses, or of the late War.
Your pardon—you do n't talk." Grant never spoke.

Perhaps he had not time to speak, before
A charming clamor spread from East to West;
Sublime in furs and jewels, at the door
Broke brightly in earth's beautiful Oppressed!

"You want your New Year presents, do you not?—
Ribbons, and rings, and lots of baby toys?"
"We want the Right of Suffrage, that is what!"
They answered, with a scornful, mighty noise.

"With Train, the chivalrous, and precious Mill,
    Woman, the great Superior of Man"——
"Hush, pretty dears, you shall have what you will—
    That is, I mean, I 'll help you if I can!"

A DOUBT.

IT is subtle, and weary, and wide;
It measures the world at my side;
It touches the stars and the sun;
It creeps with the dew to my feet;
It broods on the blossoms, and none,
Because of its brooding, are sweet;
It slides as a snake in the grass,
Whenever, wherever I pass.

It is blown to the South with the bird;
At the North, through the snow, it is heard;
With the moon from the chasms of night

It rises, forlorn and afraid;
  If I turn to the left or the right
I can not forget or evade;
When it shakes at my sleep as a dream,
If I shudder, it stifles my scream.

It smiles from the cradle; it lies
On the dust of the grave, and it cries
  In the winds and the waters; it slips
In the flush of the leaf to the ground;
  It troubles the kiss at my lips;
It lends to my laughter a sound;
It makes of the picture but paint;
It unhaloes the brow of the saint.

The ermine and crown of the king,
The sword of the soldier, the ring

Of the bride, and the robe of the priest,
The gods in their prisons of stone,
The angels that sang in the East—
Yea, the cross of my Lord, it has known;
And wings there are none that can fly
From its shadow with me, till I die!

THIS WORLD.

WHY do we love her?—that she gave us birth?
How can we thank her for ourselves?
Are we,
The pale, weak children of her old age, worth
The light that shows———there is a mirror. See!

Why do we love her? In her withering days,
Careless or frozen-hearted, half-asleep,
She leaves us to our fierce and foolish plays,
Nor kisses off the after-tears we weep.

She lets us follow our own childish cries,
  And find strange playmates ; lets our baby hands
Reach for the red glare in the tiger's eyes,
  Or the fair snake—the rainbow of the sands.

She lets us climb, through deadly dews and vines,
  After illusive birds that nurse no song,
Or die for some faint wreath of snow, that shines
  On those great heights where gods alone belong.

Still let us love her for her lovely years.
  Yet beautiful with moonlight beauty, she
Now wonders vaguely, through forlornest tears,
  How far away her morning's sun may be.

Still let us love her. She is sad and blind,
　And with wan arms forever reaching back,
Into the dreadful dark of Space, to find
　Her radiant footsteps—that have left no track.

Still let us love her, though, indeed, she seems
　To give to our small wants small heed at best.
Let her sit muffled in her ancient dream,
　With souls of her first children at her breast.

Better she brood, with wide unshadowed eyes,
　On phantom Hebrews under phantom palms,
With phantom roses flushed, and phantom skies
　Brooding above them full of Bible calms;

Better she help the young Egyptian make
  His play-house pyramid with her fancy's hands,
Or teach his Memnon's pulseless heart to ache
  With hollow music in forgotten sands;

Better, in vanished temples, watch the Greek
  Carve his divine white toys; better she hold
The Roman's savage sword and hear the shriek,
  Than feel the silence through the silken fold;

For Antony's dusk queen to lift the snake,
  For Brutus' wife the shining death of fire—
Yea, all were better than to sit and take
  Dull honey from To-day and never tire.

So let us love her, our poor Mother yet,
  For songs, for pictures that her sons have made;
Aye, let us love her more if she forget—
  To think of us would make her shrink, afraid!

THE FLIGHT OF THE CHILDREN.

THEY fade to fairies, fade and pass
Into the dimness of the dew,
Into the greenness of the grass,
Sometimes—my pretty children do;
They wander off into the wind,
And leave me, dreaming, far behind.

Then some great grayness round me steals;
My hollow hands I faintly fold;
The awful touch of blindness seals

My glimmering eyes, and I am old—
So old I care not for my years,
So old that I have done with tears.

Soon little faces, flushed and fair,
As other faces used to be,
Climb, full of wonder, up my chair,
And whisper, while they look at me;
Till, suddenly, some timid tongue
Asks me if I were ever young.

Then, wild and beautiful like a bird,
Upon my shoulders Youth alights;
Old music from its sleep is heard;
I linger in diviner nights;

A lonesome crescent cuts the sky ;
Weird, windy shadows waver by.

One lily, yellow as the moon,
  Rises and shakes its wrinkles out ;
A red geranium follows soon,
  And breathes its haunted scents about ;
From half a century of dust
A slighted hand is wanly thrust.

Then my fair, dreary dream will pass—
  No longer young nor old am I ;
My fairies leave the dew and grass,
  Out of the wind my fairies fly ;
My own sweet children sweetly say :
"You cry sometimes—when we're away."

A MASKED BALL.

THERE, in the music strangely met,
  From lands and ages wide apart,
They came, like ghosts remembering yet
  The old sweet yearning of the heart.

What sad and shining names were heard!
  What stories swept the dust, like trains!
What minster-buried echoes stirred!
  What backward splendors, backward stains!

Still two by two, as moved by fate,
  They came from silence and from song;
The tyranny of love or hate
  With that mock-pageant passed along.

There kings and cardinals long gone
  Forgot their feuds, and joined the dance.
His Holiness himself looked on,
  With something merry in his glance.

There, priestly, yet not loath to please,
  Stood Abelard; by some sad whim,
In convent coif, poor Héloïse
  Was near, confessing—what?—to him.

There, with forlornest beauty wan,
  Young Amy Robsart walked unseen,
While my Lord Leicester's looks were on
  Elizabeth, his gracious queen.

There—though the blonde Rowena gazed,
  Gold-haired and stately, with surprise—
Jeweled and dark, Rebecca raised
  The Saxon knight half-wistful eyes.

And there, despite his inky cloak,
  The melancholy Dane seemed gay,
And to Polonius' daughter spoke
  Things Shakespeare does not have him say.

"I think," he said, "I know you by
That most fantastic wreath you wear."
She, with a little languid sigh,
Asked—if his father's ghost were there.

"That voice—though veiled, it can not hide.
One trifling favor I would ask:
Give me—Yourself."
"No, no," she cried;
"You are—a stranger in a mask."

What more? Ah, well! Ophelia fled
From Hamlet—when his mask was raised.
"I—was—mistaken," Hamlet said,
As in Ophelia's face he gazed.

Ah, in the world, as at the ball,
There is a mask that lovers wear;
We call it Youth.
But let it fall,
Then—Hamlet and Ophelia stare.

A WOMAN'S BIRTHDAY.

IT is the Summer's great last heat,
It is the Fall's first chill: they meet.
Dust in the grass, dust in the air,
Dust in the grave—and every-where!
Ah, late rose, eaten to the heart:
Ah, bird, whose southward yearnings start:
The one may fall, the other fly.
Why may not I? Why may not I?

Oh, Life! that gave me for my dower
The hushing song, the worm-gnawed flower,

Let drop the rose from your shrunk breast
And blow the bird to some warm nest;
Flush out your dying colors fast:
The last dead leaf—will be the last.
No? Must I wear your piteous smile
A little while, a little while?

The withering world accepts her fate
Of mist and moaning, soon or late;
She had the dew, the scent, the spring
And upward rapture of the wing;
Their time is gone, and with it they.
And am I wooing Youth to stay
In these dry days, that still would be
Not fair to me, not fair to me?

If Time has stained with gold the hair,
Should he not gather grayness there?
Whatever gifts he chose to make,
If he has given, shall he not take?
His hollow hand has room for all
The beauty of the world to fall
Therein. I give my little part
With aching heart, with aching heart.

HIS SHARE AND MINE.

HE went from me so softly and so soon.
His sweet hands rest at morning and at noon;

The only task God gave them was to hold
A few faint rose-buds—and be white and cold.

His share of flowers he took with him away;
No more will blossom here so fair as they.

His share of thorns he left—and if they tear
My hands instead of his, I do not care.

His sweet eyes were so clear and lovely, but
To look into the world's wild light and shut:

Down in the dust they have their share of sleep;
Their share of tears is left for me to weep.

His sweet mouth had its share of kisses—Oh!
What love, what anguish, will he ever know?

Its share of thirst and murmuring and moan
And cries unsatisfied shall be my own.

He had his share of Summer. Bird and dew
Were here with him—with him they vanished to

His share of dying leaves and rains and frost
I take, with every dreary thing he lost.

The phantom of the cloud he did not see
Forevermore shall overshadow me.

He, in return, with small, still, snowy feet
Touched the Dim Path and made its Twilight sweet.

LIFE OR LOVE.

"OH, world so beautiful, could we hide
Somewhere in your flowers from death!'
A wandering voice in a palace sighed,
Where the East-rose draws her breath.

"Ah, jewels have passed through yon fires of mine,
Worth Persia ten times told;
And the essence that makes our dust divine
Is here in this cup of gold:"

And the Master knelt with a beard that rushed
  To his feet like a storm of snow.
But Youth in his bosom yearned and flushed,
  And Youth in his voice spake low.

Yet the queen lay dark on the gorgeous floor,
  With her eyes hid in her hair.
"Should she lift her face from the dust any more,"
  They moaned, "it will not be fair:

"All night, with the moon, she watches and weeps;
  No song in her ear is sweet.
All day, like the dead king's shadow, she keeps
  Her place at the dead king's feet."

"Your beauty is worth all other things
The insolent gods have seen.
It should not fade—for a thousand kings.
You shall be forever the queen."

And closer the Master held the charm:
"It is Life, O queen, that I bring."
She reached the cup with a wandering arm:
"Is it Life—for my lord, the king?"

"Nay, the king will not drink wine to-day.
There is one drop here—for you.
Oh, listen, and keep your beauty, I pray,
While the sweet world keeps the dew.

"For you new lovers shall always rise;"
And the lords and the princes near,
With the sunrise-light in their Persian eyes,
Stood, jeweled and still, to hear.

"Oh, what were Life to the lonely—what?
It is Love I would have you bring,
And Love in this widowed world is not.
Let me go to my lord, the king."

THE DEAD BOOK.

AH! from the yellow pages Time has torn
The wonder-pictures seen by clearer eyes,
And from the withered words the soul is worn.
Kiss the dead Book, and leave it where it lies.

Kiss the dead Book, and leave it in its place—
Youth's breathless bloom and dusty dreams among.
I read, where shining poems show no grace,
This dreary line, "You are no longer young."

www.ingramcontent.com/pod-product-compliance
Lightning Source LLC
LaVergne TN
LVHW011224110826
845150LV00006B/1544

* 9 7 8 1 4 2 5 5 1 5 0 5 8 *